WEBSITE IN A DAY

Creating your Wordpress Website | Patricia Redmond

Website in a Day

Additional tips and tools available at:

www.TotalOnlineMethod.com

PREFACE

This workbook is your guide to creating your first website. As a new business owner, *you* are the best salesperson for your product or service and no webmaster can capture and present the benefits of your product and your enthusiasm better than you can.

This workbook will give you the tools you need to become your own webmaster. You'll take control of your website and make changes when you want and how you want and as often as you want with-out spending a fortune or depending on someone else's schedule. Furthermore, you will be amazed at how simple it is to take total control of your website and create your most cost effective marketing tool for your new business.

- Everything you need to get started is at:

  http://www.TotalOnlineMethod.com

- No coding or complex technical skills needed
- *You* are the Webmaster! No need to depend on others to make changes to keep your site up to date
- *You* will have your own business domain name with unlimited email accounts.
- No 3-page pre-fab websites or sub domains of other sites.
- *You* will take control of your most cost-effective marketing tool!

So follow the steps outlined in this workbook and in just a few hours, you will have your own professional website published on the World Wide Web! You will find the website creation experience simple and enjoy-able and you may even decide to create several different websites, each with a different purpose or mission.

Now... let's get started!

CONTENTS

Preface 3

Why Wordpress?..................... 5

Choosing your Domain 8

Securing your Hosting 9

Installing Wordpress........... 16

Configuring your Site 23

Adding a Page....................... 30

Adding a Post........................ 32

Adding Media........................ 34

Widgets 42

Plugins................................... 45

What Now? 53

Appendix 54

WHY WORDPRESS?

Create a website with a blogging platform? Of course you can and millions do! Wordpress is much more than just a blogging platform. If you still see it that way, you will change your point of view after seeing these great sites using Wordpress.

- **The Ford Story** (http://www.thefordstory.com)
- **WSJ. Magazine** (http://magazine.wsj.com)
- **Forbes Blogs** (http://wordpress.org/showcase/forbes-blogs)

Here are plenty of reasons why you should create you website(s) using the Wordpress platform. Here are just a few:

1. It's FREE!

Wordpress is an Open Source project, which means there are hundreds of people all over the world working on it. (More than most commercial platforms.) It also means you are free to use it for any-thing from your cat's home page to a Fortune 500 web site without paying anyone a license fee and a number of other important freedoms.

Notes:

----

2. Wordpress is completely customizable and can be used for almost anything.

Wordpress is infinitely extensible. One of the core philosophies of Wordpress is to keep the core code as light and fast as possible but to provide a rich framework for the huge community to expand what Wordpress can do, limited only by their imagination.

Plugins
Plugins can extend Wordpress to do almost anything you can imagine, in the directory you can find, download, rate, and comment on all the best plugins.

Themes
Find just the right look for your website. Wordpress comes with a full theme system which makes designing everything from the simplest blog to the most complicated webzine a piece of cake, and you can even have multiple themes with totally different looks that you switch with a single click. Have a new design every day.

WordPress Ideas
The Wordpress idea forum is where you can suggest and vote on ideas for where Wordpress should go next. Wordpress is implementing the most popular features from the suggested ideas. The future is in your hands.

Notes:

----

3. Wordpress can be used for any kind of website or blog

Wordpress started as just a blogging system, but has evolved to be used as full content management system and so much more through the thousands of plugins, widgets, and themes, Wordpress is limited only by your imagination. Create an online catalogue, a sales page, an ecommerce site or one of each for your business!

4. Work from anywhere!

There is no need to be a slave to your work PC. With a Wordpress site, you can log in from anywhere and edit, create, comment and make any changes to your website anytime . . . anywhere!

5. No rebuilding

Changes you make to your templates or entries are reflected immediately on your site, with no need for regenerating static pages.

6. It's simple!

You'll have to see it to believe it. . . so let's get started creating your website!

First, we'll select your website domain.

Notes:

CHOOSING YOUR DOMAIN

Your domain name is kind of like your phone number on the World Wide Web. It's where people can find you and your company's information. Like a phone number, you would want it to be easy to re-member and easy to find so you will want to consider a few things when deciding on a domain name.

5 Tips for selecting a great domain name:

1. Keep your domain name short and easy to spell and type.
2. Include words in your domain name that you would expect people to use in a search for your product or service.
3. Avoid hyphens, underscores and other forms of punctuation in your domain name.
4. Avoid plurals if the singular is available.
5. Select a .com extension. . . .com is always the first extension that most people try when searching for a website.

Once you've decided on a few alternatives it's time to secure your web hosting and check your domains for availability.

Notes:

SECURING YOUR HOSTING

Think of your hosting account as a piece of real estate out on the World Wide Web that you will purchase to store the content of your website. Selecting a good hosting company can be confusing and a poor selection can be a real headache if you decide to move your website to another hosting company. Uptime, ease of use, 24-hour support is just a few of the features you should demand of your hosting company.

Here are a few of the hosting companies that have numerous features available on the Control Panel:

1. Bluehost.
2. HostGator
3. JustHost
4. HostMonster

My favorite for all around service, features, uptime and price is Bluehost. We'll take a look at Bluehost's sign up procedure, but they'll all be somewhat similar.

Notes:

Follow these steps to set up your account:

1. Click the "Sign up Now" button on the Bluehost home page.

Notes:

----

2. Enter your desired domain name in the "I Need a Domain Name" box.

3. Once you have identified an available domain name, go ahead and complete the sign up form to have immediate access to your hosting control panel.

Notes:

----

4. Now, log into your control panel (you will receive an email confirmation with your login information) and create an email account(s).

Notes:

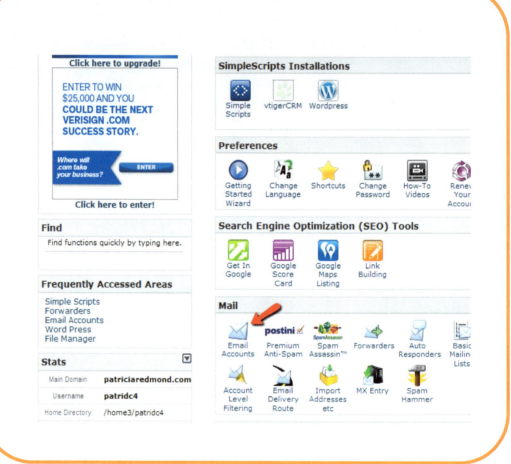

Notes:

You're now ready to install Wordpress on your site!

Notes:

- -

- -

- -

- -

INSTALLING WORDPRESS

Installing Wordpress through your Bluehost control panel is literally a 30-second process! Just a few clicks and you're done.

1. Begin by selecting the Wordpress (under the SimpleScripts Installations) icon from your control panel.

Notes:

----

2. Next, install a brand new version:

WordPress Support Options

- Official Site>
- Documentation>
- Support Forums>
- Donate to WordPress>
- Read Reviews about WordPress> on HotScripts
- Custom Web Design> for WordPress

Install WordPress

By clicking Install/Import below, you accept the SimpleScripts Terms of

a brand new version   an

Article: Creating a Website using SimpleScripts>

Notes:

----

3. Finally, leave the extension box empty, check the terms and conditions agreement box and complete the installation:

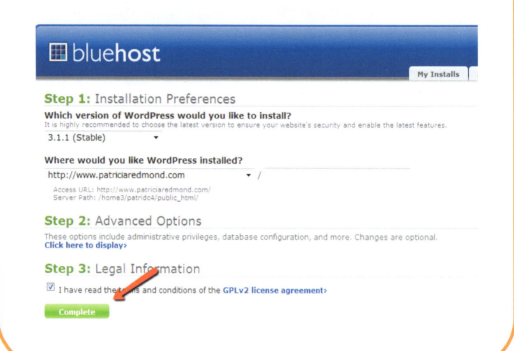

Notes:

----

4. Wordpress will automatically install in about 30 seconds and you'll receive your login information (you'll also receive an email with your login information). Immediately select and copy the password and login to your new site using the password provided. Once logged in, we'll change the password to something that you can remember.

Notes:

5. The first thing you'll want to do is change your password to something that you can remember. Click on "users" to change your password:

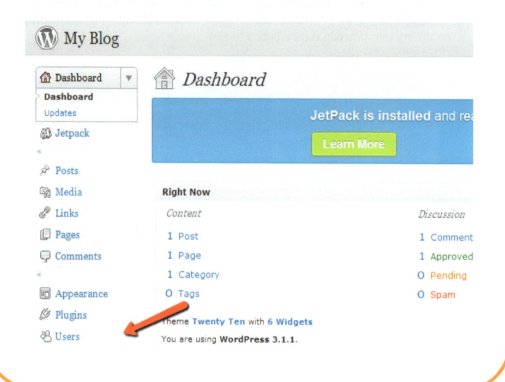

Notes:

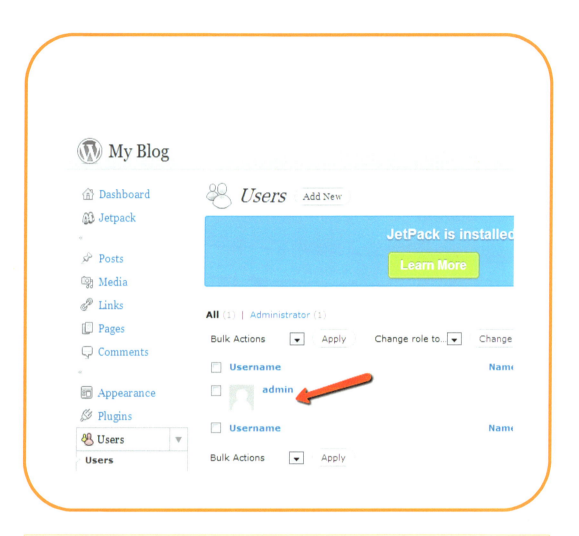

Notes:

E-mail *(required)*   your email @youremail.com

Website

AIM

Yahoo IM

Jabber / Google Talk

About Yourself

Biographical Info

Share a little biographical information

New Password   If you would like

Type your new password again.

Strength indicator   Hint: The password should be at least seven characters
^ &).

Update Profile

Enter your preferred password twice and update your profile.

That's it! Now it's time to configure your site. . .

Notes:

CONFIGURING YOUR SITE

Now, just make a couple of tweaks and your new website will begin to take shape.

1. First, go to the general settings page.

2. Next customize your settings in a couple of places:

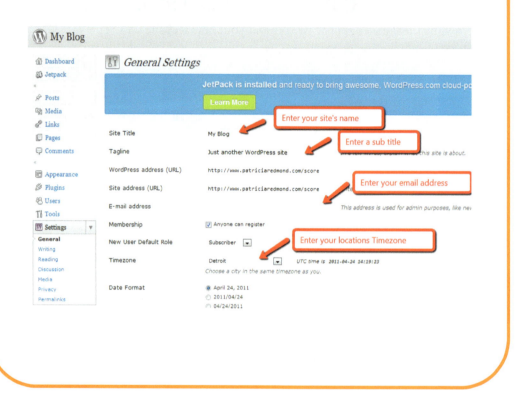

Notes:

----

3. Return to the Dashboard and click on *Permalinks*:

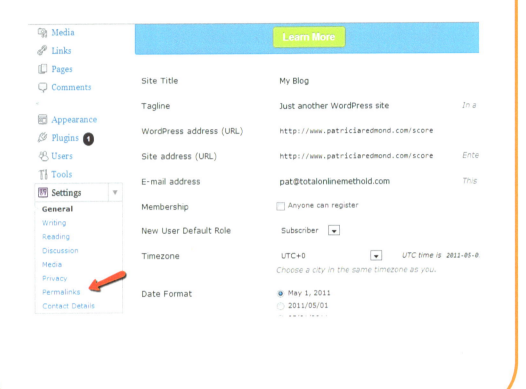

Notes:

----

4. Enter a custom structure: /%postname%/ and save:

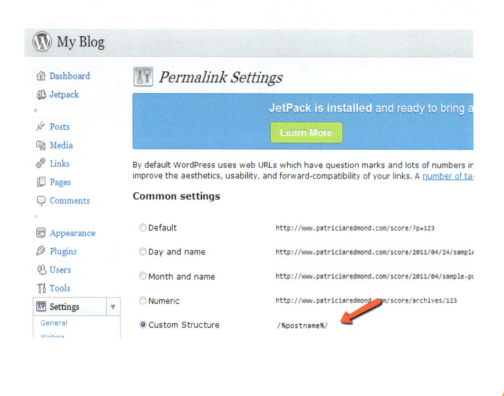

Notes:

----

5. O.K. Now let's choose a theme for your site. Return to the dashboard and select Themes from the Appearance heading:

Notes:

----

6. This is where you'll determine the "look and feel" of your site. This is one of the greatest features of Wordpress. Unlike traditional website platforms, you can change your theme at any time (Yes, even after months of content have been entered!) with just a click of your mouse and without losing any content or your search engine positions! You can choose one of the installed themes (there may only be one), or you can install a new theme. You may want to install several and preview each of them before selecting your theme.

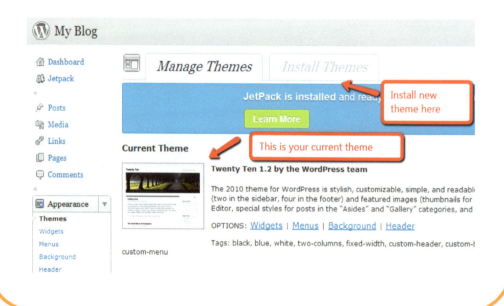

Notes:

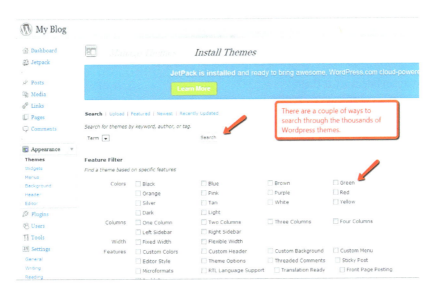

Preview and install any of thousands of Wordpress themes. New themes are added daily and you can always come back and add more themes. Once your choice(s) have been installed, just activate your favorite!

7. Now look at your site by clicking on your website's name in the upper left hand corner of your dashboard. If you're not happy with the look, just activate another theme! It's that simple.

Now you're ready to add a page. . .

Notes:

ADDING A PAGE

Characteristics of a Page

1. Static
2. Displayed independently of post history
3. Not related to categories or tags
4. Do not appear in RSS feed
5. May have sub-page

Notes:

You can also add sub-pages by selecting a "parent" for your page. Your pages are the more permanent structure of your website and should be used to publish information that doesn't change much:

- Home
- About us
- Articles
- Contact Us

Notes:

ADDING A POST

Characteristics of a Post

1. Dynamic
2. Updated on a regular basis
3. Generally current news
4. Displayed in reverse chronological order
5. Appear in RSS feed
6. Can be assigned to categories and tags

To add a post:

Notes:

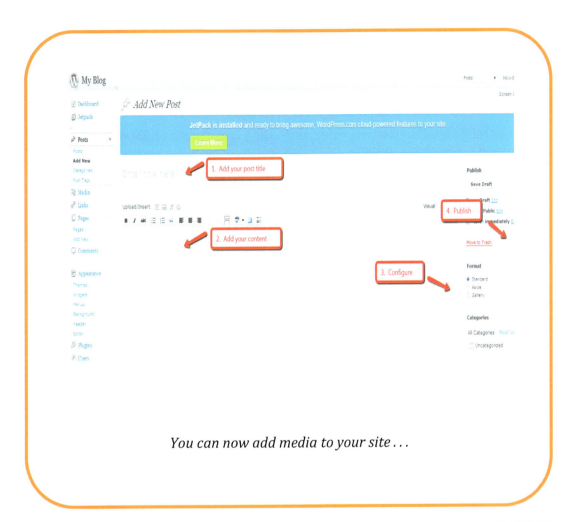

You can now add media to your site . . .

Notes:

- -

- -

- -

- -

ADDING MEDIA

You can add media (pictures, video, audio, etc.) from the media library or from the post or page itself.

First we'll look at the Media Library:

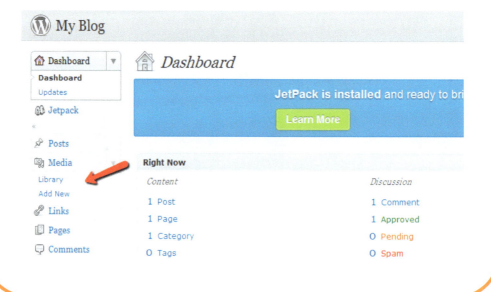

Notes:

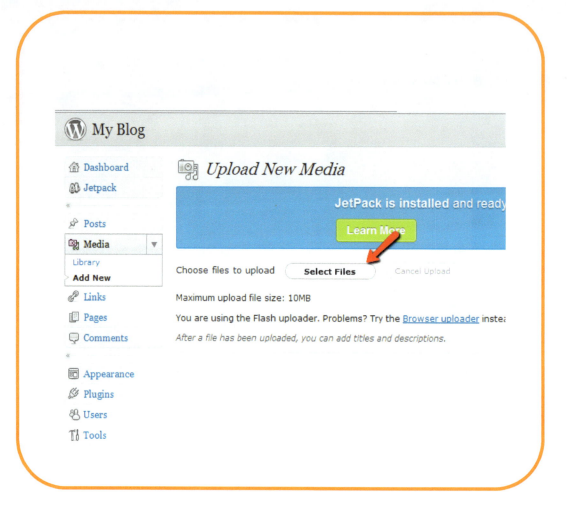

Notes:

Choose files to upload **Select Files** ~~Cancel Upload~~

Maximum upload file size: 10MB

You are using the Flash uploader. Problems? Try the Browser uploader instead.

After a file has been uploaded, you can add titles and descriptions.

Hide

File name: ant-carrying-a-box.jpg

File type: image/jpeg

Upload date: April 24, 2011

Dimensions: 170 × 227

Edit Image

Title   *   ant-carrying-a-box

Alternate Text
                            Alt text for the image, e.g. "The Mona Lisa"

Caption

Description

File URL   http://www.patriciaredmond.com/score/wp-content/uploads/2011/04/a
                    Location of the uploaded file.
                    Delete

Save all changes

Notes:

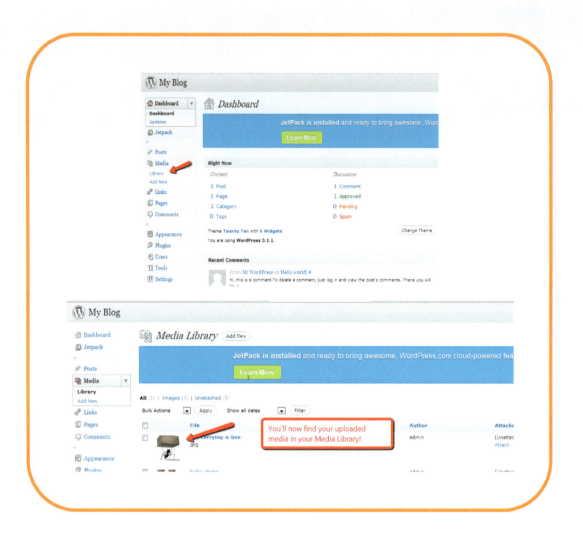

You'll now find your uploaded media in your Media Library!

Notes:

Adding media from a page or post:

W My Blog

- Dashboard
- Jetpack

Posts ▼
- Posts
- **Add New**
- Categories
- Post Tags

- Media
  - Library
  - Add New
- Links
- Pages
- Comments

- Appearance
- Plugins
- Users
- Tools

Add New Post

JetPack is installed and ready to bring awes

Learn More

Enter title here

Select the type of media you'd like to add to your post.

Upload/Insert

B *I* ABC

Notes:

Add an Image

From Computer   From URL   Media Library

Select where you'd like to upload your media file from.

Add media files from your computer

Choose files to upload   **Select Files**   Cancel Upload

Maximum upload file size: 10MB

You are using the Flash uploader. Problems? Try the Browser uploader instead.

After a file has been uploaded, you can add titles and descriptions.

Notes:

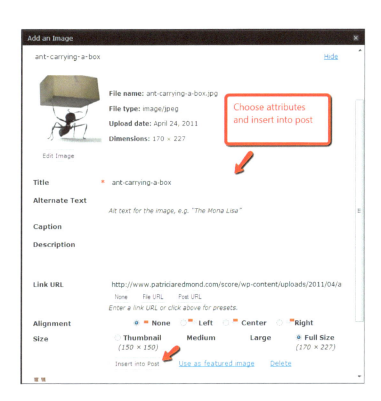

That was easy! Now let's play with the widgets...

Notes:

- -

- -

- -

- -

WIDGETS

While a theme will change the look and feel of your website, a widget will allow you to add content to your site and display it in the widgetized section (usually the sidebar) using a drag and drop method.

The WordPress community has developed a large and growing collection of widgets that will allow you to plug all sorts of things into your WordPress sidebar. From Flickr photos to your Twitter status, if there's something you'd like to add to your blog sidebar, chances are there's a widget to help you do it.

By dragging a widget to the sidebar, the new content will replace the default boxes installed by the theme. Some plugins act as widgets so you can install new widgets through the plugin menu by selecting the tag "widget."

Notes:

My Blog

Dashboard
Jetpack

Posts
Media
Links
Pages
Comments

Appearance
Themes
Widgets
Menus
Background
Header
Editor
Plugins
Users
Tools
Settings

Add New Post

JetPack is installed and ready to bring awesome, WordPress.
Learn More

Enter title here

Upload/Insert

B I ABC

Select widgets from the drop-down menu under Appearance.

Notes:

- -

- -

- -

- -

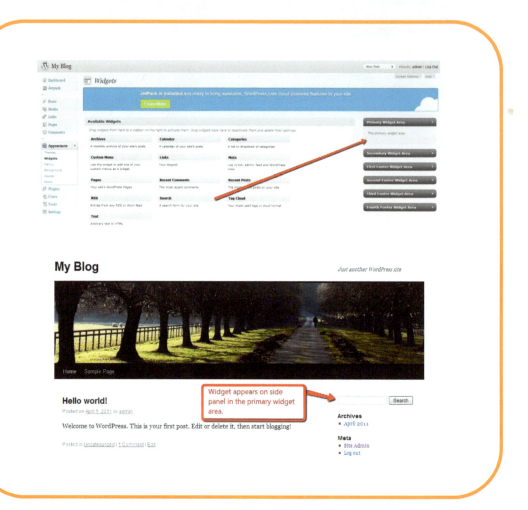

Notes:

- -

- -

- -

- -

PLUGINS

The plugins feature of Wordpress allows you to extend the capabilities of your site, and add additional features that don't exist in the standard Wordpress installation without being a programmer.

What can you do with a WordPress plugin? Just about anything. There are plugins to block spam, help you publish a podcast, and to improve the performance of your WordPress blog. If you have some specific need that is not yet accommodated by the core WordPress code-base, chances are there is a plugin to meet your needs.

How to search for and install a plugin:

Notes:

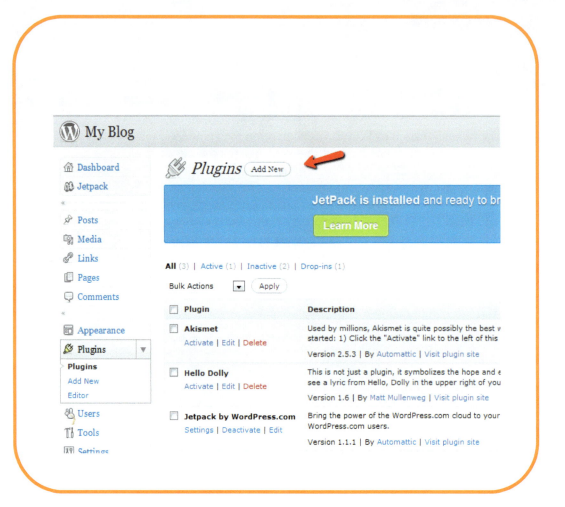

Notes:

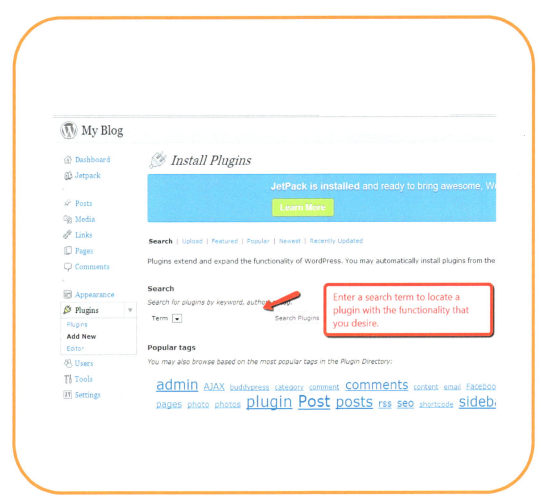

Notes:

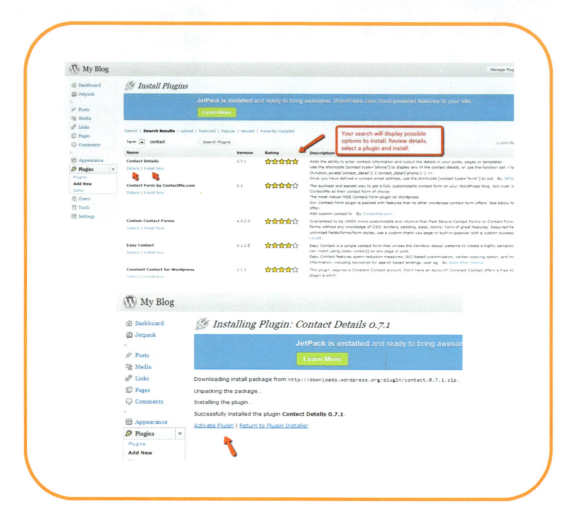

Notes:

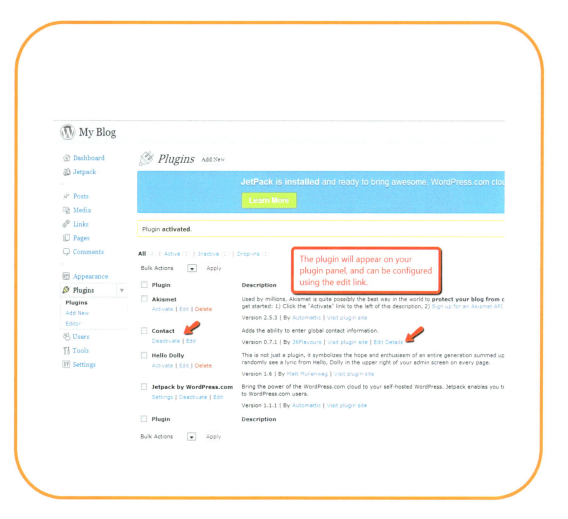

Notes:

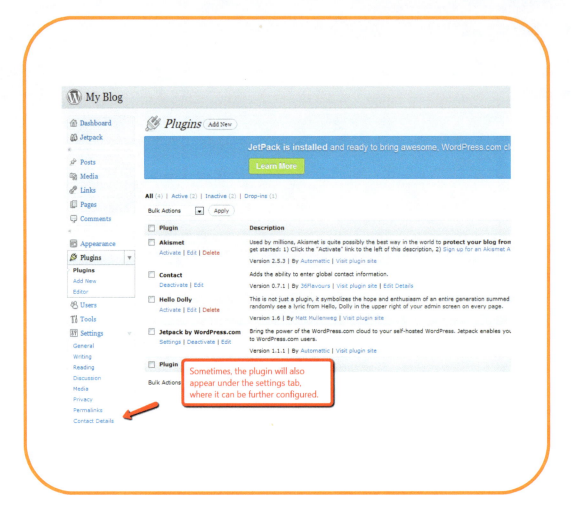

Sometimes, the plugin will also appear under the settings tab, where it can be further configured.

Notes:

Notes:

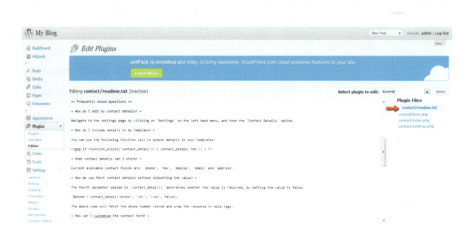

Congratulations! You just installed a new plugin and the process is the same for any plugin you may want to add to increase the functionality of your site.

You have completed the basics of your new website!

Notes:

WHAT NOW?

Now you've learned everything you need to build your own professional website. You know how to choose a domain, install Wordpress on a hosting site, select a theme, write posts and pages and customize your site with widgets and plugins.

It's time to play! Get creative and have fun. Nothing you do can't be "undone," so have a blast.

And here's more good news. . .

I'm confident that you'll enjoy building your website so much, that you'll want to create additional websites for yourself, your business, your friends and maybe even for profit! With your Bluehost web-hosting account, you can create *as many sites and add as many Wordpress installations as you would like.* You will only pay for your domain name.

So go ahead. Get started and I will bet once you get going you may even forget to eat or sleep! And when you're ready to learn more ways to use your new website to market your business, visit:

www.TotalOnlineMethod.com

for tips, tools and strategies to maximize your new website's marketing potential.

Notes:

APPENDIX

Favorite Plugins

- **Contact Form 7**
- **Really Simple CAPTCHA**
- **Suckerfish Dropdown Menu**
- **Follow Me Plugin**
- **WenderHost Subpages widget**
- **WP-Table Reloaded**
- **Google News**
- **cbnet Favicon**
- **Custom Post Background**
- **Smart YouTube**
- **Google XML Sitemaps**
- **Simple Video Embedder**
- **All in One SEO Pack**
- **cbnet Favicon**
- **W3 Total Cache**
- **CalculatorPro Calculators**
- **All in one Favicon**
- **Featured Content Gallery**
- **AddToAny: Share/Bookmark/Email Button**

Notes:

Favorite Themes
- **Thematic**
- **Minicard**
- **Wordsmith Blog**
- **Webbutveckling**
- **Future Day**
- **Blu eez**
- **Buddymatic**
- **Classroom Blog**
- **intrepidity**
- **Evolve**
- [Add your favorite]
- [Add your favorite]

More Tools
- **ThemeHeaders (http://www.themeheaders.com)**
- **WordPress Theme Generator (http://wordpressthemegen.com)**

Notes:

----

www.ingramcontent.com/pod-product-compliance
Lightning Source LLC
Chambersburg PA
CBHW050937060326
40689CB00040B/624